Why Is This Sex Book Different From All Other Sex Books?

A Parent's Guide to Embracing Sexuality Through Jewish Wisdom

Meryl Slipakoff Cohen, M.Ed., LCSW

ISBN: 978-1-4834-3792-7 (sc)
ISBN: 978-1-4834-3793-4 (e)

Because of the dynamic nature of the Internet, any web addresses or links contained in
this book may have changed since publication and may no longer be valid. The views
expressed in this work are solely those of the author and do not necessarily reflect the
views of the publisher, and the publisher hereby disclaims any responsibility for them.

Any people depicted in stock imagery provided by Thinkstock are models,
and such images are being used for illustrative purposes only.
Certain stock imagery © Thinkstock.

Lulu Publishing Services rev. date: 09/22/2015

Table of Contents

Introduction

It is not a secret that Jewish institutions are struggling to instill Jewish identity and Jewish pride in our youth. One great way to deepen Jewish youths' understanding of their heritage would be to tap into our traditions of sexual learning. There are some amazing lessons right at our fingertips—and they provide a wonderful buffer to our sexually permissive and confusing secular culture. Judaism is one of the most positive religions on sexuality, and it gives language that is both responsible and reassuring, both moral and sane. Sex sells everything else, so why not use it to sell Jewish identity?

For the last 30 years, I have been teaching and counseling professionals, educators, parents, and young people about sexuality. As a secular sexuality trainer, educator, and therapist, I've always tried to be open, honest and balanced in discussing sex, love, and relationships. I've consistently denounced the unrealistic "just say no" programs taught in the majority of American schools the last few decades. Since, as I like to quote, "more vows of abstinence break than condoms," I've instead focused on providing young people medically accurate information and the tools they need to make healthy choices.

But even the better sex-ed programs leave the values part of the discussion to the family—as they should. Our society is an amalgam of different cultures and moral values, and it's the parents who are responsible for passing on their own beliefs to their children. Unfortunately, many parents—including Jewish ones—get embarrassed and conflicted when having discussions about sexuality and sexual health.

When it came to raising my own children, I, too, struggled with how to talk about sexuality. The facts and biology presented no problem for me, but I wanted the advice I gave to be in line with Judaism's teachings. When I set out to discover what exactly those were, I was dismayed to find that most synagogues were often silent on the subject of sexuality. But I discovered that all the answers and moral footing I'd been seeking were right there in Judaism. Judaism teaches, for example, that the body was made in wisdom and is never a source of shame, but that we must always respect the distinction between public and private. It teaches that we must treat all people with dignity, and never objectify or take advantage of another human being. It teaches that all sexual relationships should be built on mutual esteem, trust, faithfulness, and an intention of permanence and that honesty should be the basis of all ethical human relationships.

Why Is This Sex Book Different From All Other Sex Books? is my attempt to take Judaism's sex-positive values and apply them to our modern world—a world in which it's just not practical, realistic, or even always valuable to assume our children will wait until marriage to have sex. This book is for parents of all ages of children, from infants to high school, to tackle the age-old questions all children ask, like: Where do I come from? Is masturbation OK? Why is my body changing? Am I normal? When is it OK to have sex? How do I know when I'm in love? Why do you get to do it and not me? I think I may be gay; what should I do?

Since in our tradition, the Jewish studies of young children prepare them for Bar and Bat Mitzvah and beyond, I concentrate in this guide my guidance for parents on preparing and getting youth through puberty. My full instruction for helping parents get through the teen years is beyond the scope of this guide.

I wrote this to help Jewish families talk with pride about our heritage and the wisdom it brings to informing our daily decisions and discourse. This guide is different because Judaism is different. King Solomon's *Song of Songs* is a perfect example of our appreciation for sensuality and the beauty that our bodies can bring. The Hebrew word "yada" means "sex," but also means "to know." We do not separate the body from the soul, and we encourage the total knowing that comes with sexual relationships. What a religion! Our heritage has beautiful answers. A religion so grounded in sexual wisdom—the Jewish mandate, for example, that the husband "arrange it so that the wife attains sexual satisfaction first" and that conjugal relations "dissipates melancholy, soothes nervousness and temper and gladdens the soul"—is a religion that deserves its sexual wisdom to be told *l'dor vador.*

A favorite teaching comes from the Daily Prayer book thanking God who has "formed us in wisdom, and created in us many orifices and vessels. It is known that if one of these be opened, or one of these be closed, it would be impossible to exist and stand before thee." Being grateful for the goodness of our bodies, helps us teach our children the importance of healthy behaviors to protect this gift.

I want this guide to chart the conversations all Jewish parents wished they'd had with their own parents. We can all lean on, and learn from, Jewish wisdom to teach kids about responsible sexual decision-making. You might already be incorporating Jewish values into your day-to-day life without acknowledging or even really understanding their roots in Judaism. You, too, can use this framework to guide these essential discussions with your family as well as to bolster your children's pride in their Jewish heritage.

Each section contains sample family discussion points for different ages of children and a "reboot" section in which parents examine their own values, memories, and preconceptions about sexuality. By drawing on Jewish teachings, we'll elevate the "sex talk" into a lifelong exchange that informs the way parents talk with their children about *all* topics.

Judaism is a lot about storytelling, and so, in a sense, is sex education. Every year at Passover, we tell the same story of the Exodus from Egypt. There's one version for the simple child, another for the irreverent child, the wise child, and the child who doesn't even understand what's going on. Our children at their various ages are like the four children: We need to give them the same information, but in different terms depending on their stage of life. We are, essentially, telling them the same story year in and year out, from generation to generation. But the *way* we tell the story—the words we use, and the child listening to those words—is in a constant state of flux. As the rabbis have long known, some children are curious and have lots of questions; others are equally curious but may be too shy to ask. It is our job, as the Torah tells us, to answer our children's questions whether they've asked them or not.

1

Jewish Values and the Six Points

The core Jewish values identified by the Central Conference of American Rabbis are useful to our understanding of sexuality. I've distilled these and other relevant values into what I call the "six points," which to me encapsulate some of the most relatable Jewish teachings that can help us talk to our children about sex.

The six points around which we'll be building these ongoing dialogues with our children are:

1) **Health** (*B'ri-ut*): Our physical, emotional and spiritual health is irrevocably tied to our sexual health. Our tradition teaches us to rejoice in and responsibly take care of our bodies.

2) **Relationships**: The family (*Mishpacha*) is the cornerstone of Jewish life, but all of our relationships should be grounded in truth (*Emet*) and honesty. Whether with our families, friends or

our romantic partners, we must express love (*Ahava*) with caring, support and empathy.

3) **Identity** (*B'tzelem Elohim*): The inherent dignity and equality of every person requires us to treat ourselves and others with respect and always to protect individual integrity.

4) **Modesty** (*Tz'niyut*): Judaism teaches that while the human body is never a source of shame or embarrassment, we should behave (and dress) in a way that respects the differences between public and private. This value obligates us to treat our bodies with humility and discipline while respecting everyone's right to privacy.

5) **Justice** (*Mishpat*): Especially because Jews have been so persecuted in the past, we must strive to treat everyone with dignity, and to work for equality and justice wherever people are treated unfairly.

6) **Joy** (*Simcha*): Sexual intimacy can bring intense physical pleasures, but these should only be enjoyed in healthy, responsible, mutually respectful relationships.

Taken all together, these six values form a very familiar star:

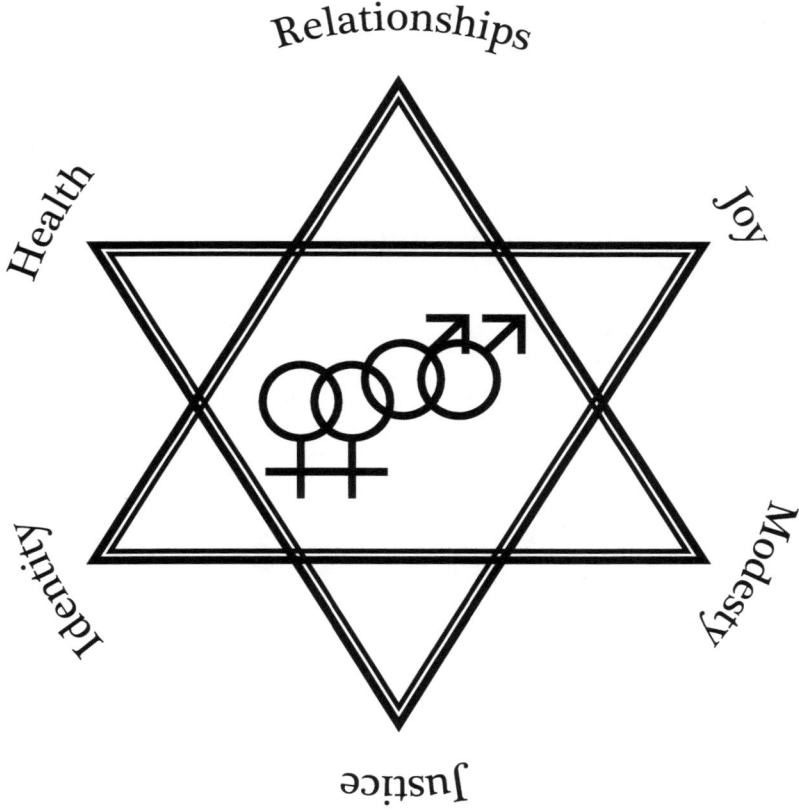

I use our six-pointed star to break down these values and explore their various applications in the context of children's physical, sexual, emotional, and moral development. **JUSTICE**, for example, is our entry into talking about bullying, date rape, and sexual harassment. **RELATIONSHIPS** covers everything from the characteristics young children value in their first friends to how romantic partners should treat each other. **IDENTITY** is a conduit, in early childhood, for talking about gender roles—questioning early on why certain colors and activities are reserved for boys or girls—and later sexual orientation and gender identity and expression. There are opportunities for discussions about gratitude for the **JOY** we receive from our own bodies and the bodies of others with an emphasis on the importance of maintaining the **HEALTH** of our precious bodies. **MODESTY** and privacy lessons within the family and outside world are ways to explore dress, the use of social media, and the concept of personal rules that will evolve as children mature.

I have used these values and the star with 7th and 8th grade students as part of a sexuality curriculum. In the class evaluations, eighty to ninety percent consistently said that the values made them proud to be Jewish and gave them guidance on making sexual decisions.

2

Early Childhood

The six points, in little-kid language, start the lifelong process of making everyday moments teachable. From a moral-reasoning standpoint, young children are extremely self-centered, unable to consider anyone else's point of view. They are also exceedingly literal—and as parents, we must use this literalism to our advantage in launching the crucial early conversations about sexuality. **Health** is central to this life phase, when we teach younger children about some of the physical mechanisms of sexuality: the proper names for body parts, including reproductive organs; where babies come from; the importance of cleanliness and hygiene.

This is the age to begin the talk about consensual body rights—teaching children to respect other people's space, not to touch anyone (or be touched) without permission. The distinction between public and private—a major principle of Judaism—becomes important here. Why can children run around naked at home but not at school? Take masturbation: While it's totally normal, natural, and enjoyable, it's something that we only do in private. We must also address gender roles and expressions in these years, when many children are spoon-fed gender stereotypes before they even start preschool. As with everything, a foundation of Jewish learning will help us examine and question the lessons of our confusing culture.

From my own parenting years,

I'll never forget when the preschool called to tell me that my daughter had fallen off her trike and told the teacher that she'd hurt her labia. "So should I come get her?" I asked. The teacher said no, so I asked why she'd called me. There was a pause. "Well... I just wanted you to know that she said 'labia.'" That afternoon, I had to explain to my 3-year-old that maybe we should just call that whole area the "vagina" at school—I didn't think the preschool was ready for vulva. But the vulva, vagina, penis, and scrotum are all body parts just like the toes, eyes, and nose, so why not teach them with equal ease and composure? They knew Volvo but vulva – not yet.

Sample Discussion Points

What is this bag under my penis? What's it for?
The bag is called the scrotum. It holds two round things called testes or testicles. They make sperm so that men can help make babies.

How are babies made?
The mother and the father get together to make a baby. You know how we learned that men have a penis and women have a vagina? Well, his penis and her vagina come together, so the sperm can go from his penis to join her egg inside. That's how a baby starts. Or if that feels like too much – how about at least saying, the man gives the sperm and the woman gives the egg and they mix it together to make a baby.

Why doesn't the baby have a penis? Was it cut off?

No, it wasn't. Girls are not born with a penis. They have other things inside like a vagina for making babies and a urethra for making pee or urine. Boys do those things with a penis. Girls have a very special place inside called the uterus where a baby can grow. Aren't all bodies wonderful!

Reboot Questions

Ask yourself:

Do I encourage my child to ask questions? Do I let him know all questions are welcome? Do I use silly names for body parts and functions? Do I check for misconceptions she may have?

Remembering your sexual messages and learning as a child helps you understand yourself: Can you remember what messages you got about masturbation? Did anyone tell you it is normal to feel JOY in touching your own body and that it is perfectly normal?

How was nudity handled? Children become modest at different ages, and respecting the privacy of the most modest child is a lesson in MODESTY.

What were the names your family used for "private" parts?

Children will always have silly names, but having the correct terms sends a signal that this is something we talk about in our family.

3

Early Elementary

By the time they're six, most children understand which topics we're comfortable discussing and which we'd rather avoid. But it isn't too late to start being askable! Kids at this age will be naturally curious about where babies come from and want more (or repeated) information on this all-important topic. Just remember that it's like the Passover story: We have to tell it every year, and realize children hear it differently at each telling.

Already, your children have a sense of themselves in relation to society, and our investment in open communication about sexuality will start to pay off. If we have established that we are a safe place to ask questions and a trusted source of information, our children will be receptive to our values. They'll also experience less anxiety about their sexual curiosity and continue to have a positive view and healthy respect toward sexuality. Listen to their questions and answer them honestly and simply. Children will also become more private during these years, and parents must learn to respect the boundaries of the most modest child. At this age, parents might institute a knock-before-entering policy to allow for privacy in the home and respect for modesty.

Now that our children are in the larger world, we must directly address sexual abuse with them so that they know how to stay safe. Explain that we value trusting relationships but not all people can be trusted. There are people out there who may want to harm them, which is why they should never hesitate to speak up if someone asks them to do something that gives them a yucky feeling. We can help our children stay safe if they know we will never be angry at them no matter what they tell us.

Being askable means being someone that stays calm enough to listen, courageous enough to respond, and emotionally available enough to see what isn't said. We can encourage and reinforce our values by playing a weekly game by asking, "What silly or funny sex ideas did the kids talk about this week?

Sample Discussion Points

"Where do I come from?"

You will hear this question over and over in these years. If your children haven't already asked it by around first grade and surely by third, find an opportunity to ask *them*: How do you think babies are made? Listen carefully to their interpretation and use their answers to correct any misinformation. You can say to your children, "When a man and woman have intercourse, a sperm cell from the man's body may join an ovum, or egg cell, made by the woman's body. The egg is as small as a speck of sand. This is how a baby starts. When a man and woman want to be very close with each other in a special, loving way, the man puts his penis into the woman's vagina. That's called sexual intercourse." Most children will squeal "yuck!" and you can say, "It does sound yucky, but when you're grown up, you will see it differently."

"Why can't I say dickhead"?

Parents are often upset when children bring home dirty or silly words from school. Rather than yell or punish them, take the opportunity to be honest and tell them some words are funny when used in private, but it is not polite to use them in public. Come on, they are funny!

"What does 'gay' mean? Is it bad?"

By this age, children will be confused by their crushes on teachers and friends. If we let them know very early on that some people will love and want to marry people of the same gender, our children will be able to come to us with their concerns and questions. If we hear "gay" used in a derogatory way, we must take advantage of the teachable moment. Point out people you know and love in the LGBTQ community and never allow hateful jesting in your home. "As I have taught you, we all deserve dignity and respect. You know how cousin Jane lives with and loves Mary? Well, they are in a homosexual relationship—some people call that gay. It is not bad at all—they are happy and love one another. I don't want you to ever use the word in an ugly way. OK?"

Reboot Questions

 Do you remember childhood sex play?

When were you aware of your sexual orientation? Were you ever confused by it?

What sexual misinformation did you have at this age, and was there anyone you could approach for clarification? Why or why not?

Am I able to react calmly, or do I always react with shock and dismay when my child tells me things that upset me?

4

Puberty

THE AGE

In Jewish tradition, the Bar or Bat Mitzvah marks a child's official passage into adulthood—and it also (not at all coincidentally) corresponds with the age when our cuddly children seem to transform into unrecognizable adults. As the old saying goes, for a decade you've been raising a dog—a devoted, sweet, submissive companion—and one day you wake up with a cat: a fiercely independent, frequently vanishing, and altogether unknowable creature who will tolerate you only on his terms.

In these crucial years, preteens are excruciatingly uncomfortable in their rapidly changing bodies, and though terrified they can't wait to grow up.

The Bar Mitzvah ceremony brilliantly symbolizes what can feel like a disconcertingly dramatic transition for many parents. At age 12 or 13, the child stands before a congregation with the same equality as a rabbi. Leading the congregation in prayer can bring an amazing sense of empowerment to a 13 year-old—and if it's done correctly, in the context of a wider understanding of Jewish values, it can also help both you and your preteen navigate some of the toughest years of a child's sexual development.

These days, the Bar Mitzvah ceremony (and all the expensive hoopla surrounding it) can also put in stark relief just how fast our kids are growing up compared to previous generations. Just look at the photos commemorating the event that appear in Jewish papers. Some girls are wearing revealing dresses, with lots of makeup, and we could mistake them for college students. They are becoming increasingly sexualized at a much earlier age. At every Bar or Bat Mitzvah, preteen party guests are kissing, some of them pairing off for more extensive explorations in the stairwell. That means we need to have already been talking to them about these issues for years by the time they reach this crucial crossroads.

Whether you're talking to your preteen about these issues or remaining uncomfortably silent, the transformation from child to adult is taking place at a breakneck pace. Preteens are being pressured to grow up earlier than ever, which puts parents in an especially delicate position. The average age for first sexual intercourse is 16 for boys and 17 for girls, which means that by 12 and 13 some preteens have already engaged in some sexual experimentation. We may not be able to stop this experimentation—and as most parents learn early on, outright forbidding children to engage in certain behaviors tends to backfire—but we can give our preteens the context for behaving appropriately and navigating this sea of changes with equanimity and maturity.

Do NOT wait until now to begin talking to them about sexuality. By talking about sex, you're not encouraging your children to engage in it. The opposite is true: research repeatedly tells us that kids who talk with their parents about sex and contraception are more likely to postpone sexual involvement and be responsible once they initiate that activity. Talking before they are actually involved in the behavior helps!

Having these conversations regularly, whenever the opportunity arises, is similar to the ongoing, multiyear process of preparing for a Bar Mitzvah ceremony. Neither should be a one-off, but rather a lifelong process of learning. If your child has only been introduced to Jewish values in preparation for the big event, and if your family stops attending temple or seldom mentions Judaism again afterward, the ceremony will lose much of its significance. Your children will have a blowout party and then be out the door, never to return to a synagogue until they have their own kids, and the cycle will start again. Instead, if you talk about sexuality and Jewish values in tandem, you can prepare them for the emotional roller coaster to come, laying the groundwork for a less tumultuous experience of puberty while instilling a positive Jewish and sexual identity.

WHAT'S HAPPENING PHYSICALLY?

Aside from the first year of life, there's no period of more rapid physical growth than early puberty. From the outset, your kids need to understand that these changes are all a normal part of growing up, even if the transformations happen for different people at a different pace.

Most kids grow several inches during this period, girls earlier than boys. Girls are, in fact, about two years ahead of boys across the board at this age, which causes insecurities for both sexes.

Sexual organs mature, and pubic hair appears. Boys often get facial hair as well during this time. Girls start wanting to shave their legs and today there will be the discussion of Brazil waxes to address even at this early age. I will stay out of your family's pubic hair debate, but it is normal and healthy to have pubic hair and getting rid of the hair is a high maintenance endeavor. Today labiaplasty ads are in many magazines, so the importance of discussing the diverse appearance of different girls' labias will help diffuse anxiety about what is and what is not normal. It's *all* normal!

Female breasts develop asymmetrically, and girls' bodies become curvier and more adult, often abruptly. Since breast cancer is so much in the news these days, preteens need to be reassured that the breast buds are normal bumps that appear way before the fatty tissue. Again, a discussion about the diverse sizes and shapes of breasts will help normalize the variety and beauty of our bodies.

It's also important to remember that the prefrontal cortex is still developing, which means preteens lack the same degree of impulse control as adults. Now that we realize the brain is maturing even into the twenties, we need to be explicit in our conversations and role play situations where our children need to detect and protect themselves from harm.

WHAT'S HAPPENING EMOTIONALLY?

During these tumultuous years when bodies are changing so rapidly, we want to protect them and make them feel normal while honoring their strong desire for independence and their sudden impatience to grow up (and away from their parents).

Peer pressure becomes more prevalent in these years. Most preteens are desperate to fit in with their peers and have a horror of standing out. Their world of friends will expose them to the choices that every day test their own personal values. As parents, we need to help our children choose a personal code of behavior concerning sex and drugs while helping them understand how to protect that code against the influence of others. Let them know they can always use you as an excuse for any challenge they encounter. That means remaining "askable" and nonthreatening as the person they can count on.

Preteens develop extremely intense friendships, particularly with members of the same sex. Know who these friends are, and open your home and activities to these important friends. The more you observe your child's interactions, the more you can comment on and influence the choices your "almost teen" is making. It's particularly important to do this right at the time that our kids are experiencing violent mood swings and massive insecurities about being abnormal, awkward, and ugly.

Our children need us most at the time they are becoming obsessed with privacy and being "left alone." Recognizing both that their feelings are normal and that our fears and anxieties are normal is a crucial first step in learning new ways to talk and LISTEN to our little cat who used to be a little puppy.

WHAT'S HAPPENING SEXUALLY?

As their hormones surge, some preteens develop their first strong sexual feelings, while others are not aware of any arousal until many years later. Your job is to explain that sexual arousal is normal, and that it's also normal to experience erections, butterflies in their tummy, wetness in their panties. They can recognize and enjoy these remarkable sensations without acting on them. Learning about sexual arousal and knowing you do not have to act on the arousal is a critical life lesson that is important to instill in these years.

Boys experience intense embarrassment over erections and difficulty understanding what they mean. It is simply arousal sometimes and hormones doing their own thing other times. It will all calm down as the years roll on.

A way to learn more about sexual arousal is masturbation. Though many children masturbate throughout their childhood, it takes on a new meaning as their bodies mature. Actually, some young children have orgasms way before puberty. Others are learning about this intense feeling for the first time.

They privately wonder if these feelings (and their private methods of dealing with them) are normal. This is their private world, but we can universalize the normalcy and beauty of privately knowing our own bodies. Without asking about their experiences with masturbation, we can say that many people enjoy touching their penis or vulva for pleasure and many do not. It is normal if you do and normal if you don't—either way, it won't harm you.

Unknown to us, preteens are privately developing strong crushes on and experiencing sexual feelings for opposite-sex and same-sex peers. Remember your first strong attractions? Even if they weren't known to that other person, they were intense and confusing. Normalize these feelings without interrogating your preteen. Tell about romantic crushes you or your friends had and how much it hurt not to have the feeling returned. Without telling about your sexual experiences, talk about how you wish someone had told you that these feelings in the body that make us feel like touching or kissing are good feelings and we can enjoy them, knowing it is normal. But acting on these feelings—kissing and touching—is quite another matter. Be aware that some preteens start dating and "hooking up" at this age. Quite a few of them have already started kissing, petting, outercourse, and even intercourse—yes, even nice Jewish kids.

By this age, parents might consider having a discussion about choosing a Personal Rule about who it is ok to kiss, how much you would be willing to let someone hug you, touch your breasts, penis, or vulva and how you would negotiate out of situations that might lead to you breaking that rule. By letting them know you are aware kids are making these decisions, you become a safe person to talk to about how hard it can be when peer pressure is dictating so much of their behavior.

INCORPORATING THE VALUES

There is so much going on during these confusing years that it can be hard to get a handle on what to say and where to start. That's why it's so much easier to have started the conversation years earlier, when your devoted canine offspring still hung on your every word.

Value 1: Health

The most important thing to emphasize during these years of raging hormones is that everything that is happening to preteens' bodies is totally normal and natural, even if it feels anything but. In Judaism, we are grateful for our bodies and have prayers of gratitude that each opening works. Our periods and wet dreams are a sign of the miracle of our bodies. In Judaism, we do not separate the soul and the body. Our traditional wisdom celebrates the beauty of the body, and it is all considered beautiful.

But how do we help our pubescent youth accept their bodies as good and normal when their breasts are growing and their hips are getting rounder and their skin is riddled with acne? We have to help preteens accept their own biological clock, which is on time but perhaps on a different timetable than their peers'. Keep books on puberty around your house that show images of the variation in body development ages 9-14. Robbie Harris's books are ideal.

GIRLS

Girls start their period during these years, following the monthly rhythm like the lunar cycle. Giving your daughter a pretty bracelet with a charm of the moon and an introduction to feminist liturgy at this stage can bind this miraculous passage to the knowledge that she can now create new life. I did that with my daughter, who seemed to appreciate the little "cycles and seasons" clay pottery with the charm and prayers, which she displayed on her dresser throughout her teen years. Tying the menstrual cycle to the miracle of pregnancy is about as spiritual as it gets.

Remind your daughter that the uterus builds up with tissue and blood all month in case she were to get pregnant, and her period is the sign that the uterus is shedding this extra tissue and blood because a pregnancy did not implant in the uterus. The cycle happens every month until the month she may be old enough and ready to be a parent herself. At that time, the uterus will grow with the pregnancy and there will be no menstrual cycle for nine months.

BOYS

Boys begin producing testosterone and their voices deepen. Spontaneous erections are common, and this is the peak period for wet dreams. Way before these disconcerting changes take place, boys deserve to know that they are not wetting the bed when they have a wet dream, and nor is it a sign they are sick or need to have sex! A wet dream is simply the male hormones at work, helping him develop the capacity to make semen, which is his contribution to the miracle of creating life. And of course the penis has a mind of its own at this stage, becoming erect at the most embarrassing times—also totally normal! Your son may not want a charm for a bracelet, but I know he would appreciate privacy. Masturbation increases during these years, longer showers, maybe more showers. Don't make any jokes about this privacy.

Value 2: Relationships

Just as your relationship with your kids is changing, so, too, is their relationship with their peers. Around this time, children will have crushes on their peers, either same or opposite sex. We all know the adults who ask the young person if they have a boyfriend or girlfriend way before the kid is interested in this type of pairing off. Don't push them. We all have crushes at different times.

Relationships with friends become all-consuming during these years. The Jewish values around truth, honesty, and empathy need reinforcing as cliques are forming and being accepted by peers feels most important. Young people can get so insecure that they lose sight of the right way to treat others. Reward them for reaching out to different kinds of people; use the Mitzvah project as a way to instill lifelong caring for others, *rachmones*. It is hard to forget our own insecurities when we were that age, but don't use the memory of unpleasant experiences you might've had to push your children to be popular. Today's definition of popular might (and probably does) include qualities that are not within the real values you want to teach your child. LISTEN.

Talk to your child about what makes a good friend (or a good romantic partner). Why would they want a romantic partner who doesn't have the qualities we would want in a good friend? Which characteristics do they look for? Which friends do they trust and why? Who has their back? As your children's relationships with people outside your family deepen and intensify, it's important that you stay relevant to them.

Value 3: Identity

While reminding our children of the inherent dignity of every person as they form relationships, we also must ensure that they value and protect their own individual integrity. In these years, the exposure to the pop sexual culture is constant, but for most preteens, their own experimentation is still in the future. Now is the ideal time to help them develop personal rules that constitute their own individual integrity. We cannot make those rules for them, but we can teach them the concept of having rules that they protect because the rule is one they chose and to break it is to not be true to who they want to be. Most of them will eventually challenge our rules about drug usage and sexual experimentation, but the existence of their own rules will strengthen them. Since we will not be there to protect them, consider role-playing scenarios where their rules will be tested.

Sexual and gender identity will also become more nuanced at this age, and gender-role expectations for males and females can be confusing to many preteens. Who texts first the boy or the girl? Who asks whom to dance; is it too forward for the girl to initiate? What if the boy is years away from caring about girls, or the girl is just not ready for a crush? Do we worry that our child might be gay? If so, relax. If our kids are gay, they already are by now and they will discover that about themselves on their own timetable. They need the space and assurance that they will have your love no matter what their orientation, their gender expression or their gender identity. If we constantly have expectations of their pairing off prematurely for fear they aren't popular, we may be pushing them into role-playing romances that will ultimately have negative consequences.

The media our children are exposed to is influencing their daily decisions. We need to be familiar with the media messages and consider how exposure to these messages affects our kids' values and sense of self. Luckily, they can't drive yet, so we can take advantage of the car rides to listen to their music with them and ask what some of the slang means —if nothing else, it's a fabulous way to get to know your kid and his pop-culture interests. Our kids are growing up in a secular world, and they're going to get these messages whether we approve them or not.

As always, you must always be on the lookout for teachable moments. For example, to teach my kids how the media was shaping their worldview, I would watch TV with them. My husband thought I was crazy, but I watched some really lame TV every week with my preteens and knew every character. We'd laugh at the same things, and we'd talk about the ads. "So what are they selling here? Is it the breasts or the butt or, no, wait—is that toothpaste?" I'd say, encouraging them to be critical thinkers rather than to accept wholesale whatever flashes across their screen. And don't just talk at them—ask for their opinions, too. Get a dialogue going.

All parents, if they aspire to knowing the first thing about their children, must cultivate media literacy. Ask constant questions of your kids so that kids can be aware that they're being targeted as a consumer. Why do we think we have to look/act/smell a particular way? Usually, the directives didn't come from our parents but from the media; just make sure your kids understand that distinction.

Value 4: Modesty and Privacy

Modesty is a crucial value to explore in a time when our kids are dressing like miniature adults. Twelve year-old girls walk around in high heels and extremely revealing bikinis because that's how our culture tells them to dress. Without just throwing prohibitions at them, we need to help them understand who is dictating these fashion ideals and why. How can our preteens wear stylish fashion without being immodest? Again, they should develop and defend a Personal Rule defining who they are by how they dress. Talking about that choice can be very "revealing."

Are the bodies that they see on TV totally unrealistic? Where are your kids' fashion and beauty ideals coming from? Again, talk about the media constantly because it's a constant presence in your kids' lives. Does the media seem exploitative? Why or why not?

And in the age of the Internet, we also need a really good grip on what privacy means and how to control ourselves on social media. First, parents need to monitor their children's computer use to a certain degree. How much of a filter are you using on the Internet? Where do you put the computer in your house? Do you control your kids' social media pages, or do you just trust that they're making the right choices online? When your child gets a cell phone, do you limit usage at all? Do you read text messages?

We need to be having family discussions in which we ask our kids about the dangers of exposing too much information on the Internet. What would be fair rules for monitoring social media? Ask your children first, and develop ground rules as a family. You're on the same team, though it's all too easy for preteens to forget that.

Value 5: Justice

To treat others with dignity, we must be able to identify when someone is bullying, harassing, or manipulating others into violating their Personal Rule. Kids know when they are being pressured to go against their own rules, but saying no and keeping their friends isn't easy at this age. Give them an out; role-play how they can get out of situations where someone is manipulating them or others. Mutual consent to engage in any sexual act is an important Jewish value.

Cyberbullying has made young people targets with painful consequences. In Jewish teaching, we are wrong to stand by when we see someone hurting. If our children know that others are being harassed and hurt, reward and praise them for coming forward to help someone. It is one of our deepest values, and one we must model for them throughout their lives.

Most synagogues require Bar and Bat Mitzvah candidates to do a community project. If your kids haven't been giving back to the community before they turn 13, volunteering might not feel meaningful to them now. All of these actions—like these conversations—should be part of a continuum. A Bar Mitzvah speech is a great opportunity to stand before the community and say they care about certain values—anti-bullying campaigns, for example, or human trafficking, homelessness, and gender and sexual equity. Whatever it is, by the time your child is a preteen, he will benefit by having some foundation in real-world issues that give him the empathy to relate to his larger community.

Value 6: Joy

By age 12, many children are having strong sexual feelings. Learning about arousal and romantic feelings is part of growing up, but acting on the feelings too early can bring disappointment. Let your child know that the feelings are normal, and they should enjoy them but not act on them—feelings and actions are miles apart.

To impart these lessons, we first have to talk to them honestly and without squeamishness about what exactly is happening in their bodies. Boys are getting nonstop erections, and girls have new feelings they don't understand. Sexual arousal is normal; it is healthy and good.

Though parents often want to use fear when talking about sex, kids know it can't be that dangerous or everyone wouldn't be praising it all the time. So to get them to trust you, talk about the POSITIVE aspects of sex. Don't be afraid to talk about the joy your body can bring you, but at the same time convey that it is a learned behavior and only pleasurable once you know your own body.

Sex is a powerful force that can bring great joy but also great pain and destruction. We must first learn about our own bodies before we share them with others. Touch, smell, taste, sight, sound are senses that delight us. Helping our kids learn to enjoy being in their own bodies, tasting the food they eat, enjoying their music, surrounding themselves with smells they enjoy is part of taking ownership of one's own pleasure. They will have a lifetime of learning how to share their body with someone else, but the early teen years are years to get used to their new bodies and a time to negotiate a truce in acceptance and then welcoming a positive body image.

HAVING THE CONVERSATION

If your children are asking you questions, then you know you've succeeded in being "askable." If they're not, where are they getting their information and what messages do they believe? Teachable moments are everywhere, so let's think of ways to start the conversation.

Like I said, the car is a great place to start conversations. Ask them about the lyrics of their favorite songs—not in a critical way, but as if you're genuinely interested in discovering what they hear in the song. And, as I have also mentioned, watch their shows with them to see how they respond and seek opportunities to see if they understand the nuances and messages from the show.

One big benefit of these conversations is the opportunity to set limits! Kids at this age feel loved when someone is checking up on them. Sure they have to roll their eyes and pretend to tune you out, but they are listening for you to keep trying. It is a dance of intimacy where we have to remain the pursuer to maintain the relationship. Everything else in their lives is so confusing; they need one clear adult figure, and that's you. You're not their friend, but their parent. Be there.

What if they ask you questions and you are embarrassed or don't know the answer. The Internet is a wonderful tool. Answers and advice are at your fingertips:

Websites

Answer http://.answer.rutgers.edu/
Advocates for Youth http://www.advocatesfor youth.org/
Parents, Family and Friends of Lesbians and Gays http://pflag.org/
Sexuality Information and Education Council of the United States http://www.siecus.org
Talk With Your Kids http://www.talkwithyourkids.org/
There's No Place Like Home ... for Sex Education http://www.noplacelikehome.org/
Planned Parenthood http://www.plannedparenthood.org/parents/talking-to-kids-about-sex-and-sexuality

---

What might be on their mind at this age:

What are blue balls?

Blue balls is a slang term for pain in the testicles that happens when a boy is sexually excited but doesn't ejaculate or have an orgasm. It can be uncomfortable, but it will go away without ejaculating. Some boys masturbate to relieve the discomfort. (Since I am from Texas, I almost called this book "Blue Balls in a Red State" because we cannot assume our kids are getting sex ed at school and can be quite confused!)

What is a condom?

It is a latex sheath that covers the penis when it is hard or erect and keeps sperm from getting into their partner during sex. It also protects the boy from sexually transmitted infections. Do you think it is a good idea for a guy to wear a condom? Why?

Does the pull-out method work?

It is not very good sex since we are not microwave ovens. Seriously, it is better than no protection at all but still very risky. The male dribbles before he shoots, meaning that before he cums, he cums a little bit—this is important. All guys have a pre-ejaculate that is clear and cleans out the urethra of acidic urine that might kill sperm. So before a guy ejaculates, he pre-ejaculates every time, and that pre-ejaculate can carry any sexually transmitted infection he may have as well as some sperm. Can you tell me why the pull-out method isn't very effective? That is why he must put on the condom before his penis touches his partner's genital or anal area.

Are there exercises to make my breasts bigger?

No, there aren't. Breast size is part of heredity. Just like other parts of our bodies, breasts and even vulvas come in all shapes and sizes, and no particular one is any better or worse. All bodies are beautiful, and we can all learn how to appreciate our best points. What do you like best about your body? (Besides your eyes and smile and amazing hair?)

Is it true you can't get pregnant if you have sex in the swimming pool?

No, that is not true. You can get pregnant in the pool only if you have sex in the pool or anywhere else if you do not use birth control. Water doesn't wash the sperm away. Do you know what birth control does?

What is penetration?

Penetration refers to a penis being inside someone else.

?
As you consider these unrecognizable creatures who've taken over your house, try to think back to what you were like at the same age. Close your eyes and try to remember what your room looked like at the same age. What posters did you have on your wall? What were your favorite songs and movies? Which celebrity did you have a crush on? Which teacher did you love and which one did you hate? Also try to think back to what was going on in your body and how you felt about it. Did you have acne? Did your breasts grow first, or did your voice change last? Were you the shortest or the tallest or in between? Think back to when you started your period or had embarrassing erections: Who did you talk to? What would have made it easier? What childhood stories can I tell to normalize what my child is going through?

Am I looking for opportunities to discuss the physical and emotional changes my child is going through?

Does my child know I would accept his sexual orientation no matter what?

The preteen years are a turbulent time of change and breaking away, but our kids still very much depend on us in many ways. Take advantage of this period before many of them will become sexually involved to set up a safe place to answer your preteens' questions and validate their feelings. If your child is having a Bar or Bat Mitzvah, you can use the occasion to clarify this passage not only physically and emotionally but spiritually as well.

In mystical Jewish teaching, the love of God and God's relationship to us is metaphorically taught through erotic poetry and the mandates for sexual relations in marriage. My postmodern takeaway interpretation is that to have sexual feelings is to be human and to be capable of having a deep spiritual connection to another person. Our positive position on sexuality and eroticism in Judaism lifts its importance to a spiritual realm that we can use to guide the conversation about sex out of the gutter and into Jewish life.

5

High School

Like it or not, these days, children aren't waiting till they get married to have sex. How do we deal with that? We already know that forbidding children to have sex is like willing the earth to be flat. Instead, we must go on talking with our children about the inherent dignity of every person, whether male or female, gay or transgender. Because every person deserves honor and respect, the foundation of all relationships, sexual or otherwise, should be consent, mutual esteem, as well as being honest, equal and responsible. By impressing on our children the importance of love and mutual respect in *all* relationships, we aren't pretending that they have to be married to have sex; we're telling them that they have to be serious, and to take responsibility for their choices and the consequences they might have. The values of modesty and privacy offer an effective buffer against a culture riddled by advertising objectifying the body, exploitation, and endless permutations of pornography. If we've been doing it right, we've been talking consistently with our children about media depictions for years now, but adolescence is no time to stop.

I always had a drawer of condoms in my kitchen—partly because I was out doing lectures and kept my demonstration stash there, but also because I wanted to give implicit permission for my teens to be peer educators and advocates to help their friends understand the importance of staying safe. I never worried about the mixed message that I was giving, which was: 1) I want you to wait and have meaningful, pleasurable sexual relations in a mutually exclusive relationship, but 2) if you choose to have sex, I want you to have access to and always use protection. This double message works in many contexts: I don't want you drinking, and I certainly don't want you drinking and driving, and you can always call and we will come get you without consequence. Permission? Protection? Sometimes double messages just make good sense.

Today, our teens deserve to know where to go for birth control. In Texas, we have parental consent laws for contraception, which is a hurdle teens shouldn't have to jump. A nice, cheap Hanukah present would be a signed consent form, which is another effective double message. It is not permission but rather a statement of trust that if they make a decision to have sex, they will take measures to stay safe.

At a synagogue safe-sex talk I did for graduating teens, I remember a very popular boy telling the group he wished he had been more respectful of the Jewish text concerning mutual pleasure and respecting our sexual partners. He looked back at his popularity and how available girls were to him and he regretted his behavior that never considered her needs. I adapt and paraphrase what Eugene Borowitz wrote in the 1960's about the ethical hierarchy of sexual decision making in Judaism: the highest level is sex in marriage with mutual pleasure and consent; then sex with love with mutual pleasure and consent; than sex with mutual pleasure and consent; and lastly, simply self -gratification. Helping our teens navigate sexual decision making by encouraging discussions of Jewish texts in the home and religious school will make the text relevant to their daily lives.

Discussion Points

Is oral sex,sex?

Oral sex means pleasuring a male by sucking his penis or pleasuring a female by licking or sucking her clitoris and vulva. Do you think that's sex?

If two people don't have a sexually transmitted disease, can they get it from sexual intercourse?

No. Just like the flu, you can only catch it from someone who has it. The problem is that the most common symptom of many STD's is no symptom at all.

Once people are sexually involved, they need to be screened for STD's at a clinic.

Reboot Questions

?

Do I want my teen's first sexual experience to be different than mine? How?

Will I know when my teen is having sex?

How would I respond if my teen asks, "When is it OK to have sex?"

Can I be honest about how pleasurable sexual relations can be?

Can I be honest about how unpleasable sexual relations can be?

What would I say if my teen asks me to go on birth control?

Have I talked to my teen about condoms? Why not?

Am I sure my teen understands about sexually transmitted infections, how we get pregnant, how to protect from both?

6

V'Shinantam L'Vanecha

Some extremely curious and intelligent people have mulled over these sexuality questions for centuries. In Judaism, we have these centuries of interpretations and perceptions to guide us, but the sheer volume can be dizzying. The streamlining and selection I've done might not adhere to every rabbi's standard, but then one of the most appealing features of contemporary Judaism is the value we place on questioning, and our tireless search for relevance and guidance in today's world. Rabbi simply means "teacher," and a parent is the first and most important teacher a child will ever have.

V'Shinantam L'Vanecha, teach your children well, so that they can choose healthy lives guided by Jewish values. It might feel uncomfortable at first, and take extraordinary bravery, but we should all aspire to becoming an "askable" parent, the one kids will approach with their most private, embarrassing questions—at age 2, and 8, and 20. Having these conversations, constantly and calmly requires moral courage. It's far easier just to hope our children figure out the answers themselves without getting hurt or harming others. But talking to your children about sex is every Jewish parent's obligation, like our Jewish obligation to teach them to swim: If you don't do it, they may just drown in this sex-saturated culture. Our children deserve this information, and it's our job as Jewish parents to teach them well so that they can live responsible, healthy lives.

About the Author

Meryl Slipakoff Cohen

Meryl has a private practice specializing in sexuality consulting, counseling and training. Her work focuses on enhancing sexual communication by helping: parents talk to their children about sexual health and decision making; partners enhance their sexual and sensual lives; agencies and schools teach their youth about sex education; health and social service agencies integrate and communicate a holistic model of sexual health; mature adults embrace sexuality and aging; and religious groups embrace sexuality education. She was the Vice-President of Education for Planned Parenthood Gulf Coast for several decades. She has served as faculty for several universities including, Baylor College of Medicine, University of Texas School of Public Health and currently teaches Human Sexuality at The University of Houston Graduate College of Social Work. She is a frequent lecturer for government agencies, schools, and secular and Jewish parent groups. For over 25 years, she has taught reproductive and sexual health to parents, teens, and professionals. She has been a local expert for many television programs and appeared on the *Montel Williams* show. Providing sexual and relationship counseling for over 15 years, she has helped families and couples honestly address sexual concerns. She served on the national board of the American Association of Sex Educators, Counselors and Therapists, through which she is a Certified Sex Educator. She received the McGovern Award for Community Contributions and

Activism in Health Promotion from the University of Texas School of Public Health Center for Health Promotion and Prevention Research. National Council of Jewish Women awarded her their highest honor with the Hannah Solomon Award for her work in adolescent health. Hadassah, Jewish Federation and NCJW frequently request her sexual health presentations at their meetings and installations. Meryl has a Master's Degree in Science Education from the University of Texas and a Master's Degree in Social Work from the University of Houston. She has used her sexuality expertise in her Jewish community teaching parents and fifth graders at one Houston Synagogue for over 30 years, as well as teaching parents and youth at several Jewish Day Schools. Her "Jewish wisdom through 6 Jewish values" has been used as a curriculum for 6th through 12th grade students. She can be reached at merylscohen@gmail.com.